little
explorers

Forest Magic

A Guidebook for Little Woodland Explorers

words & art by

Sarah Grindler

NIMBUS
PUBLISHING LTD.
— NIMBUS.CA —

Nimbus Publishing Limited
3660 Strawberry Hill Street, Halifax, NS, B3K 5A9
(902) 455-4286 nimbus.ca

Printed and bound in China

NB1520

Cover design: Heather Bryan
Interior design: Jenn Embree
Editor: Penelope Jackson
Editor for the press: Emily MacKinnon

Library and Archives Canada Cataloguing in Publication

Title: Forest magic : a guidebook for little woodland explorers / words & art by Sarah Grindler.
Names: Grindler, Sarah, author, illustrator.
Description: Series statement: Little explorers series
Identifiers: Canadiana (print) 20200386395 | Canadiana (ebook) 20200386409
ISBN 9781771089265 (hardcover) | ISBN 9781771085854 (EPUB)
Subjects: LCSH: Forest ecology—Juvenile literature. | LCSH: Forests and forestry—Juvenile literature.
Classification: LCC QH541.5.F6 G75 2021 | DDC j577.3—dc23

Nimbus Publishing acknowledges the financial support for its publishing activities from the Government of Canada, the Canada Council for the Arts, and from the Province of Nova Scotia. We are pleased to work in partnership with the Province of Nova Scotia to develop and promote our creative industries for the benefit of all Nova Scotians.

To my beautiful son, Jackson, and in memory of
Judy Burch—thank you for all your forest wisdom.

What do you notice when you are walking in the forest? Different types of trees? Lichens or mushrooms? Wildflowers? How about the sound of a chattering squirrel or the sweet smell of tree sap? There's so much to see, hear, touch, and smell!

Let's investigate the magic of a forest.

Have you ever heard of a nurse log? A nurse log is a fallen tree that gives life to the forest. As it slowly decays, it offers nutrients and moisture to soil, seedlings, ferns, fungi, lichen, mosses, saplings, and so much more.

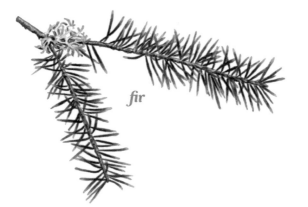

fir

maple

A healthy forest is home to a lot of different types of trees that can support each other and share nutrients through their root systems. You can get to know them by their leaves.

oak

cedar

maple keys

maple sapling

Here are some maple tree seeds (called keys), and this is a maple tree sapling. After many years, this tiny sapling will grow tall and strong.

Saplings are baby trees. They need sunlight and plenty of moisture in order to grow into beautiful, majestic giants.

**If you planted a sapling today,
would it grow faster than you?**

pileated woodpecker

Trees also create homes for so many
plants and animals.

Here is a little home in a tree trunk. Can you
guess which of these birds lives inside it?

(Hint: it sleeps during the day and is awake
at night.)

raven

Cooper's
hawk

Canada jay

barred
owl

"Hoot, hoot!" It's an owl! What other creatures can you think of that make their homes in the forest?

There are some hiding in these pages.
Can you find them?

There are creatures with no legs, two legs, four legs, six legs, eight legs, and even ones with almost one hundred legs that live in the forest!

snail

white-tailed deer

Swainson's thrush

rough-skinned newt

grey comma butterfly

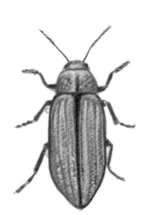

**golden buprestid beetle
(golden jewel beetle)**

**cross orbweaver
(European garden spider)**

millipede

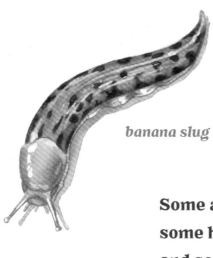

banana slug

Some are slimy, some are furry,
some have very long tongues,
and some glow like little lights.
Some sing beautiful songs and
others buzz quietly.

skunk

Columbia spotted frog

squirrel

firefly

white-tailed deer

beaver

Each creature has a part to play in keeping the balance of life in the forest's ecosystem.

American bushtit
(and nest)

Forests are also home to fungi, lichen, moss, wildflowers, and many species of plants.

The fungus on the right is called a turkey-tail mushroom. You can often find it growing on the trunk of a tree or on the side of a nurse log.

Why do you think it is called a turkey tail?

Look at this turkey's tail. Can you see the resemblance?

turkey-tail mushroom

There are so many different types of colourful and beautiful mushrooms. Some are also known as toadstools. Find them popping out of the forest floor, dotted along nurse logs, or growing up a tree. Some are brightly coloured while others blend into their surroundings.

chanterelle   *toadstool*

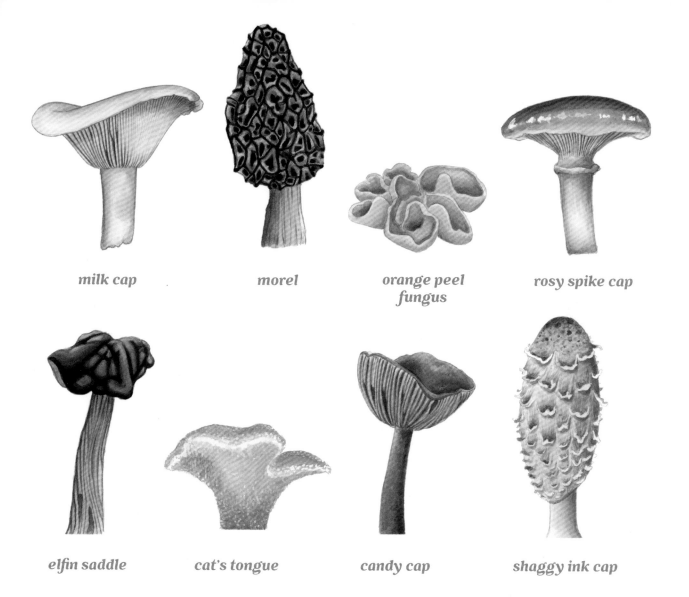

milk cap

morel

orange peel
fungus

rosy spike cap

elfin saddle

cat's tongue

candy cap

shaggy ink cap

Take a look at these colourful lichens.

Lichens are special organisms made up of different species of fungi and algae. Some look dusty or crusty, some look like tiny branches with cups, and some look like long tendrils of hair hanging from the branches of a tree.

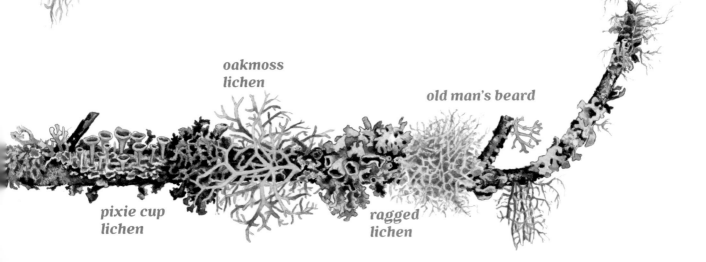

oakmoss
lichen

old man's beard

pixie cup
lichen

ragged
lichen

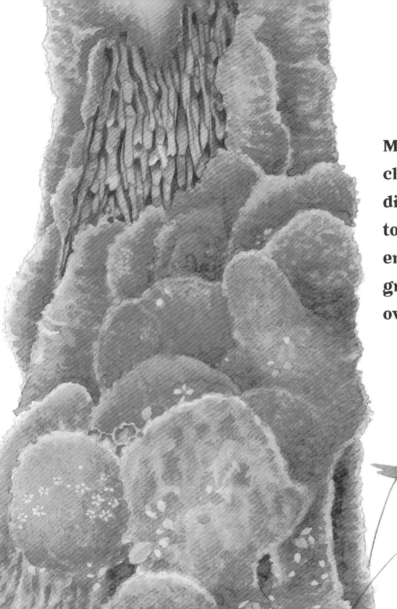

Mosses are tiny plants clustered together on many different types of surfaces to form spongy cushions or enchanting carpets of vibrant green. Moss can be found all over the planet.

In warmer months, beautiful wildflowers sprout from the forest floor and through meadows. My favourite wildflower is the Calypso orchid, also known as a fairy slipper. Many wildflowers have funny names.

Calypso orchid (fairy slipper)

foxglove

Which of these wildflowers is your favourite?

Have you ever smelled them?

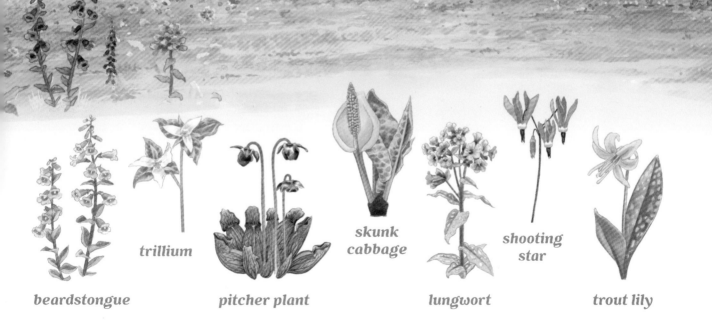

beardstongue

trillium

pitcher plant

skunk cabbage

lungwort

shooting star

trout lily

There is so much life in the forest
and so many things to explore!

Safe to touch

pine cone

ragged lichen

alder cones

What is your favourite thing to see in the forest?
To smell? To hear? To touch?

Has a grown-up shown you which things in the forest are safe to pick up?

woolly bear caterpillar

monkey flower

lungwort lichen

owl feather

Do NOT touch!

poison ivy

bird's nest

toadstool

baneberry

rough-skinned newt

What do you wish to discover on your next adventure in the forest?